Working Papers I, Chapters 1-14

to accompany

Fundamental Accounting Principles

Eleventh Edition

Kermit D. Larson
The University of Texas at Austin

William W. Pyle

1987

IRWIN

Homewood, Illinois 60430

ISBN 0-256-03583-0

1 2 3 4 5 6 7 8 9 0 VK 0 1 2 3 4 5 6 7

Contents

PROBLEM 1-1 or 1-1A

CASH	+	ACCOUNTS RECEIVABLE	+	OFFICE SUPPLIES	+	OFFICE EQUIPMENT	+	BUILDING	=	ACCOUNTS PAYABLE	+	MORTGAGE PAYABLE	+	JUNE COLE, CAPITAL
ASSETS									=	LIABILITIES			+	OWNER'S EQUITY

PROBLEM 1-2 or 1-2A

Name _____

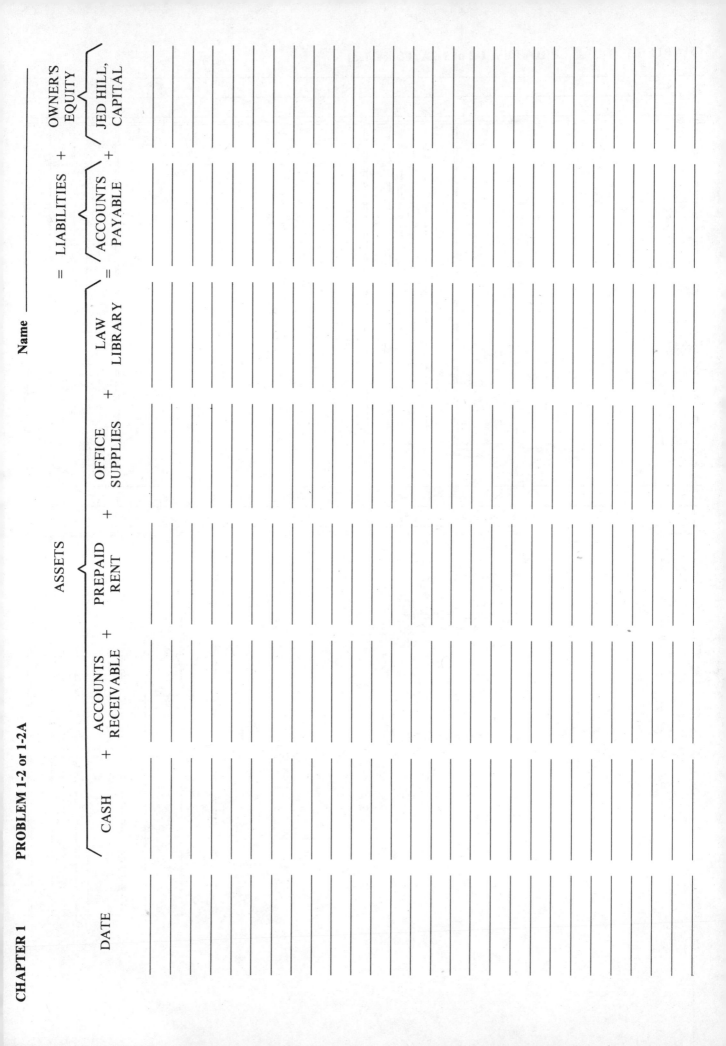

DATE	ASSETS						= LIABILITIES +	OWNER'S EQUITY
	CASH	+ ACCOUNTS RECEIVABLE	+ PREPAID RENT	+ OFFICE SUPPLIES	+ LAW LIBRARY		= ACCOUNTS PAYABLE	+ JED HILL, CAPITAL

CHAPTER 1   PROBLEM 1-4 or 1-4A   Name _____

DATE	CASH	+	ACCOUNTS RECEIVABLE	+	PREPAID RENT	+	PREPAID INSURANCE	+	DRAFTING SUPPLIES	=	ACCOUNTS PAYABLE	+	NED HALL, CAPITAL

ASSETS = LIABILITIES + OWNER'S EQUITY

Cash		Accounts Payable

Accounts Receivable		Susan Kent, Capital

Office Supplies		Susan Kent, Withdrawals

Office Equipment		Commissions Earned

Automobile		Appraisal Fees Earned

Land		Office Salaries Expense

Building		Advertising Expense

Mortgage Payable

GENERAL JOURNAL   PAGE 1

DATE	ACCOUNT TITLES AND EXPLANATION	P.R.	DEBIT	CREDIT

DATE	ACCOUNT TITLES AND EXPLANATION	P.R.	DEBIT	CREDIT

GENERAL LEDGER

Cash   ACCT. NO. 111

DATE	EXPLANATION	P.R.	DEBIT	CREDIT	BALANCE

Accounts Receivable   ACCT. NO. 112

DATE	EXPLANATION	P.R.	DEBIT	CREDIT	BALANCE

Prepaid Rent   ACCT. NO. 113

DATE	EXPLANATION	P.R.	DEBIT	CREDIT	BALANCE

Prepaid Insurance   ACCT. NO. 114

DATE	EXPLANATION	P.R.	DEBIT	CREDIT	BALANCE

Office Supplies
ACCT. NO. 115

DATE	EXPLANATION	P.R.	DEBIT	CREDIT	BALANCE

Office Equipment
ACCT. NO. 131

DATE	EXPLANATION	P.R.	DEBIT	CREDIT	BALANCE

Accounts Payable
ACCT. NO. 211

DATE	EXPLANATION	P.R.	DEBIT	CREDIT	BALANCE

Dale Hall, Capital
ACCT. NO. 311

DATE	EXPLANATION	P.R.	DEBIT	CREDIT	BALANCE

Dale Hall, Withdrawals
ACCT. NO. 312

DATE	EXPLANATION	P.R.	DEBIT	CREDIT	BALANCE

Accounting Revenue   ACCT. NO. 411

DATE	EXPLANATION	P.R.	DEBIT	CREDIT	BALANCE

Utilities Expense   ACCT. NO. 514

DATE	EXPLANATION	P.R.	DEBIT	CREDIT	BALANCE

Cash

_____|_____

Accounts Receivable

_____|_____

Prepaid Insurance

_____|_____

Office Equipment

_____|_____

Machinery

_____|_____

Building

_____|_____

Land

_____|_____

Notes Payable

_____|_____

Accounts Payable

_____|_____

Jerry Marsh, Capital

_____|_____

Jerry Marsh, Withdrawals

_____|_____

Excavating Revenue

_____|_____

Machinery Repairs Expense

_____|_____

Wages Expense

_____|_____

Machinery Rentals Expense   *Gas and Oil Expense*

GENERAL JOURNAL   **PAGE 1**

DATE	ACCOUNT TITLES AND EXPLANATION	P.R.	DEBIT	CREDIT

DATE	ACCOUNT TITLES AND EXPLANATION	P.R.	DEBIT	CREDIT

GENERAL LEDGER

Cash   ACCT. NO. 111

DATE	EXPLANATION	P.R.	DEBIT	CREDIT	BALANCE

Accounts Receivable   ACCT. NO. 112

DATE	EXPLANATION	P.R.	DEBIT	CREDIT	BALANCE

Prepaid Rent   ACCT. NO. 113

DATE	EXPLANATION	P.R.	DEBIT	CREDIT	BALANCE

Prepaid Insurance   ACCT. NO. 114

DATE	EXPLANATION	P.R.	DEBIT	CREDIT	BALANCE

Drafting Supplies   ACCT. NO. 115

DATE		EXPLANATION	P.R.	DEBIT	CREDIT	BALANCE

Office and Drafting Equipment   ACCT. NO. 131

DATE		EXPLANATION	P.R.	DEBIT	CREDIT	BALANCE

Accounts Payable   ACCT. NO. 211

DATE		EXPLANATION	P.R.	DEBIT	CREDIT	BALANCE

Nancy Ives, Capital   ACCT. NO. 311

DATE		EXPLANATION	P.R.	DEBIT	CREDIT	BALANCE

Nancy Ives, Withdrawals   ACCT. NO. 312

DATE		EXPLANATION	P.R.	DEBIT	CREDIT	BALANCE

Architectural Fees Earned   ACCT. NO. 411

DATE		EXPLANATION	P.R.	DEBIT	CREDIT	BALANCE

Salaries Expense   ACCT. NO. 511

DATE		EXPLANATION	P.R.	DEBIT	CREDIT	BALANCE

Blueprinting Expense   ACCT. NO. 512

DATE		EXPLANATION	P.R.	DEBIT	CREDIT	BALANCE

Utilities Expense   ACCT. NO. 513

DATE		EXPLANATION	P.R.	DEBIT	CREDIT	BALANCE

GENERAL JOURNAL

DATE	ACCOUNT TITLES AND EXPLANATION	P.R.	DEBIT	CREDIT

DATE		ACCOUNT TITLES AND EXPLANATION	P.R.	DEBIT	CREDIT

Cash   ACCT. NO. 111

DATE		EXPLANATION	P.R.	DEBIT	CREDIT	BALANCE

Accounts Receivable   ACCT. NO. 112

DATE		EXPLANATION	P.R.	DEBIT	CREDIT	BALANCE

Prepaid Rent   ACCT. NO. 113

DATE		EXPLANATION	P.R.	DEBIT	CREDIT	BALANCE

Prepaid Insurance   ACCT. NO. 114

DATE		EXPLANATION	P.R.	DEBIT	CREDIT	BALANCE

Office Supplies   ACCT. NO. 115

DATE		EXPLANATION	P.R.	DEBIT	CREDIT	BALANCE

Law Library   ACCT. NO. 131

DATE		EXPLANATION	P.R.	DEBIT	CREDIT	BALANCE

Accounts Payable   ACCT. NO. 211

DATE		EXPLANATION	P.R.	DEBIT	CREDIT	BALANCE

Ted Lee, Capital   ACCT. NO. 311

DATE		EXPLANATION	P.R.	DEBIT	CREDIT	BALANCE

Ted Lee, Withdrawals   ACCT. NO. 312

DATE		EXPLANATION	P.R.	DEBIT	CREDIT	BALANCE

Legal Fees Earned   ACCT. NO. 411

DATE	EXPLANATION	P.R.	DEBIT	CREDIT	BALANCE

Rent Expense   ACCT. NO. 511

DATE	EXPLANATION	P.R.	DEBIT	CREDIT	BALANCE

Salaries Expense   ACCT. NO. 512

DATE	EXPLANATION	P.R.	DEBIT	CREDIT	BALANCE

Telephone Expense   ACCT. NO. 513

DATE	EXPLANATION	P.R.	DEBIT	CREDIT	BALANCE

Insurance Expense   ACCT. NO. 514

DATE	EXPLANATION	P.R.	DEBIT	CREDIT	BALANCE

Office Supplies Expense   ACCT. NO. 515

DATE	EXPLANATION	P.R.	DEBIT	CREDIT	BALANCE

GENERAL JOURNAL

DATE	ACCOUNT TITLES AND EXPLANATION	P.R.	DEBIT	CREDIT

DATE		ACCOUNT TITLES AND EXPLANATION	P.R.	DEBIT	CREDIT	

GENERAL LEDGER

Cash

ACCT. NO. 111

DATE		EXPLANATION	P.R.	DEBIT	CREDIT	BALANCE
Dec.	31	Balance	✓			1 9 4 0 00

Accounts Receivable

ACCT. NO. 112

DATE		EXPLANATION	P.R.	DEBIT	CREDIT	BALANCE

Prepaid Insurance

ACCT. NO. 113

DATE		EXPLANATION	P.R.	DEBIT	CREDIT	BALANCE
Dec.	31	Balance	✓			9 1 5 00

Office Supplies

ACCT. NO. 114

DATE		EXPLANATION	P.R.	DEBIT	CREDIT	BALANCE
Dec.	31	Balance	✓			2 9 0 00

Office Equipment

ACCT. NO. 131

DATE		EXPLANATION	P.R.	DEBIT	CREDIT	BALANCE
Dec.	31	Balance	✓			6 2 5 0 00

Accumulated Depreciation, Office Equipment

ACCT. NO. 132

DATE		EXPLANATION	P.R.	DEBIT	CREDIT	BALANCE
Dec.	31	Balance	✔			1 9 2 0 00

Automobile

ACCT. NO. 133

DATE		EXPLANATION	P.R.	DEBIT	CREDIT	BALANCE
Dec.	31	Balance	✔			12 7 8 0 00

Accumulated Depreciation, Automobile

ACCT. NO. 134

DATE		EXPLANATION	P.R.	DEBIT	CREDIT	BALANCE
Dec.	31	Balance	✔			2 1 5 0 00

Accounts Payable

ACCT. NO. 211

DATE		EXPLANATION	P.R.	DEBIT	CREDIT	BALANCE
Dec.	31	Balance	✔			2 2 5 00

Office Salaries Payable

ACCT. NO. 212

DATE		EXPLANATION	P.R.	DEBIT	CREDIT	BALANCE

Unearned Management Fees

ACCT. NO. 213

DATE		EXPLANATION	P.R.	DEBIT	CREDIT	BALANCE
Dec.	31	Balance	✔			4 5 0 00

Dale Pitts, Capital   ACCT. NO. 311

DATE		EXPLANATION	P.R.	DEBIT	CREDIT	BALANCE
Dec.	31	Balance	√			11 1 4 5 00

Dale Pitts, Withdrawal   ACCT. NO. 312

DATE		EXPLANATION	P.R.	DEBIT	CREDIT	BALANCE
Dec.	31	Balance	√			18 6 0 0 00

Sales Commissions Earned   ACCT. NO. 411

DATE		EXPLANATION	P.R.	DEBIT	CREDIT	BALANCE
Dec.	31	Balance	√			41 2 8 0 00

Management Fees Earned   ACCT. NO. 412

DATE		EXPLANATION	P.R.	DEBIT	CREDIT	BALANCE

Office Salaries Expense   ACCT. NO. 511

DATE		EXPLANATION	P.R.	DEBIT	CREDIT	BALANCE
Dec.	31	Balance	√			10 3 0 0 00

Advertising Expense   ACCT. NO. 512

DATE		EXPLANATION	P.R.	DEBIT	CREDIT	BALANCE
Dec.	31	Balance	√			8 3 0 00

Rent Expense   ACCT. NO. 513

DATE		EXPLANATION	P.R.	DEBIT	CREDIT	BALANCE
Dec.	31	Balance	√			4 8 0 0 00

Telephone Expense   ACCT. NO. 514

DATE		EXPLANATION	P.R.	DEBIT	CREDIT	BALANCE
Dec.	31	Balance	√			4 6 5 00

Insurance Expense   ACCT. NO. 515

DATE		EXPLANATION	P.R.	DEBIT	CREDIT	BALANCE
			√			

Office Supplies Expense   ACCT. NO. 516

DATE		EXPLANATION	P.R.	DEBIT	CREDIT	BALANCE

Depreciation Expense, Office Equipment   ACCT. NO. 517

DATE		EXPLANATION	P.R.	DEBIT	CREDIT	BALANCE

Depreciation Expense, Automobile   ACCT. NO. 518

DATE		EXPLANATION	P.R.	DEBIT	CREDIT	BALANCE

GENERAL JOURNAL   PAGE 1

DATE	ACCOUNT TITLES AND EXPLANATION	P.R.	DEBIT	CREDIT

GENERAL LEDGER

Cash
ACCT. NO. 111

DATE	EXPLANATION	P.R.	DEBIT	CREDIT	BALANCE
Dec. 31	Balance	✓			2 240 00

Accounts Receivable
ACCT. NO. 112

DATE	EXPLANATION	P.R.	DEBIT	CREDIT	BALANCE
Dec. 31	Balance	✓			545 00

Prepaid Insurance
ACCT. NO. 113

DATE	EXPLANATION	P.R.	DEBIT	CREDIT	BALANCE
Dec. 31	Balance	✓			3 580 00

Office Supplies
ACCT. NO. 114

DATE	EXPLANATION	P.R.	DEBIT	CREDIT	BALANCE
Dec. 31	Balance	✓			320 00

Office Equipment
ACCT. NO. 131

DATE	EXPLANATION	P.R.	DEBIT	CREDIT	BALANCE
Dec. 31	Balance	✓			3 650 00

Accumulated Depreciation, Office Equipment
ACCT. NO. 132

DATE	EXPLANATION	P.R.	DEBIT	CREDIT	BALANCE
Dec. 31	Balance	✓			1 680 00

Trucks   ACCT. NO. 133

DATE		EXPLANATION	P.R.	DEBIT	CREDIT	BALANCE
Dec.	31	Balance	✔			44 2 0 0 00

Accumulated Depreciation, Trucks   ACCT. NO. 134

DATE		EXPLANATION	P.R.	DEBIT	CREDIT	BALANCE
Dec.	31	Balance	✔			11 5 4 0 00

Buildings   ACCT. NO. 135

DATE		EXPLANATION	P.R.	DEBIT	CREDIT	BALANCE
Dec.	31	Balance	✔			168 0 0 0 00

Accumulated Depreciation, Buildings   ACCT. NO. 136

DATE		EXPLANATION	P.R.	DEBIT	CREDIT	BALANCE
Dec.	31	Balance	✔			28 6 0 0 00

Land   ACCT. NO. 137

DATE		EXPLANATION	P.R.	DEBIT	CREDIT	BALANCE
Dec.	31	Balance	✔			17 5 0 0 00

Unearned Storage Fees   ACCT. NO. 212

DATE		EXPLANATION	P.R.	DEBIT	CREDIT	BALANCE
Dec.	31	Balance	✔			1 7 3 0 00

Salaries and Wages Payable   ACCT. NO. 213

DATE	EXPLANATION	P.R.	DEBIT	CREDIT	BALANCE

Mortgage Payable   ACCT. NO. 231

DATE	EXPLANATION	P.R.	DEBIT	CREDIT	BALANCE
Dec. 31	Balance	✓			120 0 0 0 00

John Hall, Capital   ACCT. NO. 311

DATE	EXPLANATION	P.R.	DEBIT	CREDIT	BALANCE
Dec. 31	Balance	✓			54 1 1 0 00

John Hall, Withdrawals   ACCT. NO. 312

DATE	EXPLANATION	P.R.	DEBIT	CREDIT	BALANCE
Dec. 31	Balance	✓			24 0 0 0 00

Revenue from Moving Services   ACCT. NO. 411

DATE	EXPLANATION	P.R.	DEBIT	CREDIT	BALANCE
Dec. 31	Balance	✓			90 1 1 5 00

Storage Fees Earned   ACCT. NO. 412

DATE	EXPLANATION	P.R.	DEBIT	CREDIT	BALANCE
Dec. 31	Balance	✓			7 7 7 0 00

Office Salaries Expense   ACCT. NO. 511

DATE		EXPLANATION	P.R.	DEBIT	CREDIT	BALANCE
Dec. 31	Balance		✓			11 4 0 0 00

Drivers' and Helpers' Wages Expense   ACCT. NO. 512

DATE		EXPLANATION	P.R.	DEBIT	CREDIT	BALANCE
Dec. 31	Balance		✓			26 6 3 0 00

Gas, Oil, and Repairs Expense   ACCT. NO. 513

DATE		EXPLANATION	P.R.	DEBIT	CREDIT	BALANCE
Dec. 31	Balance		✓			2 6 8 0 00

Insurance Expense   ACCT. NO. 514

DATE		EXPLANATION	P.R.	DEBIT	CREDIT	BALANCE

Office Supplies Expense   ACCT. NO. 515

DATE		EXPLANATION	P.R.	DEBIT	CREDIT	BALANCE

Depreciation Expense, Office Equipment   ACCT. NO. 516

DATE		EXPLANATION	P.R.	DEBIT	CREDIT	BALANCE

Depreciation Expense, Trucks   ACCT. NO. 517

DATE	EXPLANATION	P.R.	DEBIT	CREDIT	BALANCE

Depreciation Expense, Building   ACCT. NO. 518

DATE	EXPLANATION	P.R.	DEBIT	CREDIT	BALANCE

Mortgage Interest Expense   ACCT. NO. 519

DATE	EXPLANATION	P.R.	DEBIT	CREDIT	BALANCE
Dec. 31	Balance	✔			10 80 0 00

GENERAL JOURNAL   PAGE 1

DATE	ACCOUNT TITLES AND EXPLANATION	P.R.	DEBIT	CREDIT

GENERAL JOURNAL

DATE	ACCOUNT TITLES AND EXPLANATION	P.R.	DEBIT	CREDIT

GENERAL JOURNAL

DATE	ACCOUNT TITLES AND EXPLANATION	P.R.	DEBIT	CREDIT

DATE	ACCOUNT TITLES AND EXPLANATION	P.R.	DEBIT	CREDIT

GENERAL LEDGER

Cash   ACCT. NO. 111

DATE		EXPLANATION	P.R.	DEBIT	CREDIT	BALANCE
Dec.	31	Balance	✔			2 5 4 0 00

Accounts Receivable   ACCT. NO. 112

DATE		EXPLANATION	P.R.	DEBIT	CREDIT	BALANCE

Prepaid Insurance   ACCT. NO. 113

DATE		EXPLANATION	P.R.	DEBIT	CREDIT	BALANCE
Dec.	31	Balance	✔			1 5 2 5 00

Office Supplies   ACCT. NO. 114

DATE		EXPLANATION	P.R.	DEBIT	CREDIT	BALANCE
Dec.	31	Balance	✔			2 6 0 00

Office Equipment   ACCT. NO. 131

DATE		EXPLANATION	P.R.	DEBIT	CREDIT	BALANCE
Dec.	31	Balance	✔			2 4 5 0 00

Accumulated Depreciation, Office Equipment   ACCT. NO. 132

DATE		EXPLANATION	P.R.	DEBIT	CREDIT	BALANCE
Dec.	31	Balance	✔			8 1 5 00

Buildings and Improvements

ACCT. NO. 133

DATE		EXPLANATION	P.R.	DEBIT	CREDIT	BALANCE
Dec.	31	Balance	√			92 0 0 0 00

Accumulated Depreciation, Buildings and Improvements

ACCT. NO. 134

DATE		EXPLANATION	P.R.	DEBIT	CREDIT	BALANCE
Dec.	31	Balance	√			21 3 5 0 00

Land

ACCT. NO. 135

DATE		EXPLANATION	P.R.	DEBIT	CREDIT	BALANCE
Dec.	31	Balance	√			95 0 0 0 00

Wages Payable

ACCT. NO. 212

DATE		EXPLANATION	P.R.	DEBIT	CREDIT	BALANCE

Property Taxes Payable

ACCT. NO. 213

DATE		EXPLANATION	P.R.	DEBIT	CREDIT	BALANCE

Interest Payable

ACCT. NO. 214

DATE		EXPLANATION	P.R.	DEBIT	CREDIT	BALANCE

Unearned Rent   ACCT. NO. 215

DATE		EXPLANATION	P.R.	DEBIT	CREDIT	BALANCE
Dec.	31	Balance	√			7 8 0 00

Mortgage Payable   ACCT. NO. 231

DATE		EXPLANATION	P.R.	DEBIT	CREDIT	BALANCE
Dec.	31	Balance	√			118 0 0 0 00

June Lake, Capital   ACCT. NO. 311

DATE		EXPLANATION	P.R.	DEBIT	CREDIT	BALANCE
Dec.	31	Balance	√			41 8 1 0 00

June Lake, Withdrawals   ACCT. NO. 312

DATE		EXPLANATION	P.R.	DEBIT	CREDIT	BALANCE
Dec.	31	Balance	√			18 2 0 0 00

Rent Earned   ACCT. NO. 411

DATE		EXPLANATION	P.R.	DEBIT	CREDIT	BALANCE
Dec.	31	Balance	√			51 8 6 5 00

Wages Expense   ACCT. NO. 511

DATE		EXPLANATION	P.R.	DEBIT	CREDIT	BALANCE
Dec.	31	Balance	√			10 1 2 0 00

Utilities Expense   ACCT. NO. 512

DATE		EXPLANATION	P.R.	DEBIT	CREDIT	BALANCE
Dec.	31	Balance	✓			8 2 5 00

Property Taxes Expense   ACCT. NO. 513

DATE		EXPLANATION	P.R.	DEBIT	CREDIT	BALANCE
Dec.	31	Balance	✓			1 9 6 5 00

Insurance Expense   ACCT. NO. 514

DATE		EXPLANATION	P.R.	DEBIT	CREDIT	BALANCE

Office Supplies Expense   ACCT. NO. 515

DATE		EXPLANATION	P.R.	DEBIT	CREDIT	BALANCE

Depreciation Expense, Office Equipment   ACCT. NO. 516

DATE		EXPLANATION	P.R.	DEBIT	CREDIT	BALANCE

Depreciation Expense, Buildings and Improvements   ACCT. NO. 517

DATE		EXPLANATION	P.R.	DEBIT	CREDIT	BALANCE

Interest Expense

ACCT. NO. 518

DATE		EXPLANATION	P.R.	DEBIT	CREDIT	BALANCE
Dec.	31	Balance	✔			9 7 3 5 00

GENERAL JOURNAL

DATE	ACCOUNT TITLES AND EXPLANATION	P.R.	DEBIT	CREDIT

DATE	ACCOUNT TITLES AND EXPLANATION	P.R.	DEBIT	CREDIT

(The work sheet for this problem is in the back of this booklet.)

GENERAL JOURNAL

DATE	ACCOUNT TITLES AND EXPLANATION	P.R.	DEBIT	CREDIT

DATE	ACCOUNT TITLES AND EXPLANATION	P.R.	DEBIT	CREDIT

GENERAL JOURNAL   **PAGE 1**

DATE	ACCOUNT TITLES AND EXPLANATION	P.R.	DEBIT	CREDIT

DATE		ACCOUNT TITLES AND EXPLANATION	P.R.	DEBIT	CREDIT

DATE	ACCOUNT TITLES AND EXPLANATION	P.R.	DEBIT	CREDIT

DATE		ACCOUNT TITLES AND EXPLANATION	P.R.	DEBIT	CREDIT

GENERAL LEDGER

Cash   ACCT. NO. 111

DATE	EXPLANATION	P.R.	DEBIT	CREDIT	BALANCE

Prepaid Insurance   ACCT. NO. 113

DATE	EXPLANATION	P.R.	DEBIT	CREDIT	BALANCE

Office Supplies   ACCT. NO. 114

DATE	EXPLANATION	P.R.	DEBIT	CREDIT	BALANCE

Automobile
ACCT. NO. 131

DATE		EXPLANATION	P.R.	DEBIT	CREDIT	BALANCE

Accumulated Depreciation, Automobile
ACCT. NO. 132

DATE		EXPLANATION	P.R.	DEBIT	CREDIT	BALANCE

Salaries Payable
ACCT. NO. 213

DATE		EXPLANATION	P.R.	DEBIT	CREDIT	BALANCE

Sue Gage, Capital
ACCT. NO. 311

DATE		EXPLANATION	P.R.	DEBIT	CREDIT	BALANCE

Sue Gage, Withdrawals
ACCT. NO. 312

DATE		EXPLANATION	P.R.	DEBIT	CREDIT	BALANCE

Income Summary
ACCT. NO. 313

DATE		EXPLANATION	P.R.	DEBIT	CREDIT	BALANCE

Commissions Earned

ACCT. NO. 411

DATE		EXPLANATION	P.R.	DEBIT	CREDIT	BALANCE

Rent Expense

ACCT. NO. 511

DATE		EXPLANATION	P.R.	DEBIT	CREDIT	BALANCE

Salaries Expense

ACCT. NO. 512

DATE		EXPLANATION	P.R.	DEBIT	CREDIT	BALANCE

Gas, Oil, and Repairs Expense

ACCT. NO. 513

DATE		EXPLANATION	P.R.	DEBIT	CREDIT	BALANCE

Telephone Expense   ACCT. NO. 514

DATE	EXPLANATION	P.R.	DEBIT	CREDIT	BALANCE

Insurance Expense   ACCT. NO. 515

DATE	EXPLANATION	P.R.	DEBIT	CREDIT	BALANCE

Office Supplies Expense   ACCT. NO. 516

DATE	EXPLANATION	P.R.	DEBIT	CREDIT	BALANCE

Depreciation Expense, Automobile   ACCT. NO. 517

DATE	EXPLANATION	P.R.	DEBIT	CREDIT	BALANCE

SUE GAGE REALTY

Work Sheet for Month Ended May 31, 19___

ACCOUNT TITLES	TRIAL BALANCE		ADJUSTMENTS		ADJUSTED TRIAL BALANCE		INCOME STATEMENT		BALANCE SHEET	
	DR.	CR.	DR.	CR.	DR.	CR.	DR.	CR.	DR.	CR.

SUE GAGE REALTY
Income Statement
For Month Ended May 31, 19___

SUE GAGE REALTY
Post-Closing Trial Balance
May 31, 19___

SUE GAGE REALTY
Balance Sheet
May 31, 19___

SUE GAGE REALTY

Work Sheet for Month Ended June 30, 19___

ACCOUNT TITLES	TRIAL BALANCE		ADJUSTMENTS		ADJUSTED TRIAL BALANCE		INCOME STATEMENT		BALANCE SHEET	
	DR.	CR.	DR.	CR.	DR.	CR.	DR.	CR.	DR.	CR.

SUE GAGE REALTY
Income Statement
For Month Ended June 30, 19___

SUE GAGE REALTY
Post-Closing Trial Balance
June 30, 19___

SUE GAGE REALTY
Balance Sheet
June 30, 19___

(The work sheet for this problem is in the back of this booklet.)

Cash   ACCT. NO. 111

DATE	EXPLANATION	P.R.	DEBIT	CREDIT	BALANCE
Dec. 31	Balance	✔			7 7 5 00

Bowling Supplies   ACCT. NO. 112

DATE	EXPLANATION	P.R.	DEBIT	CREDIT	BALANCE
Dec. 31	Balance	✔			1 4 2 0 00

Prepaid Insurance   ACCT. NO. 113

DATE	EXPLANATION	P.R.	DEBIT	CREDIT	BALANCE
Dec. 31	Balance	✔			1 3 3 5 00

Prepaid Interest   ACCT. NO. 114

DATE	EXPLANATION	P.R.	DEBIT	CREDIT	BALANCE

Bowling Equipment   ACCT. NO. 131

DATE	EXPLANATION	P.R.	DEBIT	CREDIT	BALANCE
Dec. 31	Balance	✔			49 5 6 5 00

Accumulated Depreciation, Bowling Equipment   ACCT. NO. 132

DATE		EXPLANATION	P.R.	DEBIT	CREDIT	BALANCE
Dec.	31	Balance	✔			7 6 4 0 00

Accounts Payable   ACCT. NO. 211

DATE		EXPLANATION	P.R.	DEBIT	CREDIT	BALANCE
Dec.	31	Balance	✔			1 3 5 00

Wages Payable   ACCT. NO. 212

DATE	EXPLANATION	P.R.	DEBIT	CREDIT	BALANCE

Rent Payable   ACCT. NO. 213

DATE	EXPLANATION	P.R.	DEBIT	CREDIT	BALANCE

Taxes Payable   ACCT. NO. 214

DATE	EXPLANATION	P.R.	DEBIT	CREDIT	BALANCE

Mortgage Payable   ACCT. NO. 231

DATE	EXPLANATION	P.R.	DEBIT	CREDIT	BALANCE
Dec. 31	Balance	✔			10 0 0 0 00

Gary Berg, Capital   ACCT. NO. 311

DATE	EXPLANATION	P.R.	DEBIT	CREDIT	BALANCE
Dec. 31	Balance	✔			21 2 0 0 00

Gary Berg, Withdrawals   ACCT. NO. 312

DATE	EXPLANATION	P.R.	DEBIT	CREDIT	BALANCE
Dec. 31	Balance	✔			15 6 5 0 00

Income Summary   ACCT. NO. 313

DATE	EXPLANATION	P.R.	DEBIT	CREDIT	BALANCE

Bowling Revenue   ACCT. NO. 411

DATE	EXPLANATION	P.R.	DEBIT	CREDIT	BALANCE
Dec. 31	Balance	✔			54 5 0 0 00

Wages Expense

ACCT. NO. 511

DATE	EXPLANATION	P.R.	DEBIT	CREDIT	BALANCE
Dec. 31	Balance	✔			16 2 5 5 00

Equipment Repairs Expense

ACCT. NO. 512

DATE	EXPLANATION	P.R.	DEBIT	CREDIT	BALANCE
Dec. 31	Balance	✔			4 2 0 00

Rent Expense

ACCT. NO. 513

DATE	EXPLANATION	P.R.	DEBIT	CREDIT	BALANCE
Dec 31	Balance	✔			4 8 0 0 00

Utilities Expense

ACCT. NO. 514

DATE	EXPLANATION	P.R.	DEBIT	CREDIT	BALANCE
Dec. 31	Balance	✔			2 1 3 5 00

Taxes Expense

ACCT. NO. 515

DATE	EXPLANATION	P.R.	DEBIT	CREDIT	BALANCE
Dec. 31	Balance	✔			5 2 0 00

Bowling Supplies Expense

ACCT. NO. 516

DATE	EXPLANATION	P.R.	DEBIT	CREDIT	BALANCE

Insurance Expense

ACCT. NO. 517

DATE	EXPLANATION	P.R.	DEBIT	CREDIT	BALANCE

Depreciation Expense, Bowling Equipment

ACCT. NO. 518

DATE	EXPLANATION	P.R.	DEBIT	CREDIT	BALANCE

Interest Expense

ACCT. NO. 519

DATE	EXPLANATION	P.R.	DEBIT	CREDIT	BALANCE
Dec. 31	Balance	✔			6 0 0 00

LEISURE ALLEYS

Income Statement

For Year Ended December 31, 19___

LEISURE ALLEYS
Balance Sheet
December 31, 19___

LEISURE ALLEYS
Post-Closing Trial Balance
December 31, 19___

GENERAL JOURNAL   **PAGE 1**

DATE	ACCOUNT TITLES AND EXPLANATION	P.R.	DEBIT	CREDIT

DATE	ACCOUNT TITLES AND EXPLANATION	P.R.	DEBIT	CREDIT

(The work sheet for this problem is in the back of this booklet.)

Cash — ACCT. NO. 111

DATE		EXPLANATION	P.R.	DEBIT	CREDIT	BALANCE
Dec.	31	Balance	✔			5 2 5 00

Accounts Receivable — ACCT. NO. 112

DATE		EXPLANATION	P.R.	DEBIT	CREDIT	BALANCE
Dec.	31	Balance	✔			6 7 0 00

Prepaid Insurance — ACCT. NO. 113

DATE		EXPLANATION	P.R.	DEBIT	CREDIT	BALANCE
Dec.	31	Balance	✔			2 27 5 00

Office Supplies — ACCT. NO. 114

DATE		EXPLANATION	P.R.	DEBIT	CREDIT	BALANCE
Dec.	31	Balance	✔			2 4 5 00

Prepaid Rent — ACCT. NO. 115

DATE		EXPLANATION	P.R.	DEBIT	CREDIT	BALANCE
Dec.	31	Balance	✔			2 5 0 00

Office Equipment   ACCT. NO. 131

DATE		EXPLANATION	P.R.	DEBIT	CREDIT	BALANCE
Dec.	31	Balance	✔			2 4 6 0 00

Accumulated Depreciation, Office Equipment   ACCT. NO. 132

DATE		EXPLANATION	P.R.	DEBIT	CREDIT	BALANCE
Dec.	31	Balance	✔			5 7 0 00

Delivery Equipment   ACCT. NO. 133

DATE		EXPLANATION	P.R.	DEBIT	CREDIT	BALANCE
Dec.	31	Balance	✔			14 7 9 0 00

Accumulated Depreciation, Delivery Equipment   ACCT. NO. 134

DATE		EXPLANATION	P.R.	DEBIT	CREDIT	BALANCE
Dec.	31	Balance	✔			3 1 5 0 00

Accounts Payable   ACCT. NO. 211

DATE		EXPLANATION	P.R.	DEBIT	CREDIT	BALANCE
Dec.	31	Balance	✔			8 9 0 00

Rent Payable   ACCT. NO. 212

DATE	EXPLANATION	P.R.	DEBIT	CREDIT	BALANCE

Salaries and Wages Payable   ACCT. NO. 213

DATE	EXPLANATION	P.R.	DEBIT	CREDIT	BALANCE

Unearned Delivery Service Revenue   ACCT. NO. 214

DATE	EXPLANATION	P.R.	DEBIT	CREDIT	BALANCE
Dec. 31	Balance	✔			5 5 0 00

Edward Deal, Capital   ACCT. NO. 311

DATE	EXPLANATION	P.R.	DEBIT	CREDIT	BALANCE
Dec. 31	Balance				22 9 0 5 00

Edward Deal, Withdrawals   ACCT. NO. 312

DATE	EXPLANATION	P.R.	DEBIT	CREDIT	BALANCE
Dec. 31	Balance	✔			12 0 0 0 00

Income Summary

ACCT. NO. 313

DATE		EXPLANATION	P.R.	DEBIT	CREDIT	BALANCE

Delivery Service Revenue

ACCT. NO. 411

DATE		EXPLANATION	P.R.	DEBIT	CREDIT	BALANCE
Dec.	31	Balance	✓			41 5 5 5 00

Rent Expense

ACCT. NO. 511

DATE		EXPLANATION	P.R.	DEBIT	CREDIT	BALANCE
Dec.	31	Balance	✓			2 5 0 0 00

Telephone Expense

ACCT. NO. 512

DATE		EXPLANATION	P.R.	DEBIT	CREDIT	BALANCE
Dec.	31	Balance	✓			3 4 5 00

Office Salaries Expense

ACCT. NO. 513

DATE		EXPLANATION	P.R.	DEBIT	CREDIT	BALANCE
Dec.	31	Balance	✓			10 0 6 0 00

Insurance Expense, Office Equipment   ACCT. NO. 514

DATE	EXPLANATION	P.R.	DEBIT	CREDIT	BALANCE

Office Supplies Expense   ACCT. NO. 515

DATE	EXPLANATION	P.R.	DEBIT	CREDIT	BALANCE

Depreciation Expense, Office Equipment   ACCT. NO. 516

DATE	EXPLANATION	P.R.	DEBIT	CREDIT	BALANCE

Delivery Wages Expense   ACCT. NO. 517

DATE	EXPLANATION	P.R.	DEBIT	CREDIT	BALANCE
Dec. 31	Balance	✔			20 3 2 0 00

Gas, Oil, and Repairs Expense   ACCT. NO. 518

DATE	EXPLANATION	P.R.	DEBIT	CREDIT	BALANCE
Dec. 31	Balance	✔			3 1 8 0 00

Insurance Expense, Delivery Equipment

ACCT. NO. 519

DATE		EXPLANATION	P.R.	DEBIT	CREDIT	BALANCE

Depreciation Expense, Delivery Equipment

ACCT. NO. 520

DATE		EXPLANATION	P.R.	DEBIT	CREDIT	BALANCE

GENERAL JOURNAL

PAGE 1

DATE		ACCOUNT TITLES AND EXPLANATION	P.R.	DEBIT	CREDIT

DATE	ACCOUNT TITLES AND EXPLANATION	P.R.	DEBIT	CREDIT

ED'S DELIVERY SERVICE

Income Statement

For Year Ended Deccember 31, 19___

ED'S DELIVERY SERVICE
Balance Sheet
December 31, 19___

ED'S DELIVERY SERVICE
Post-Closing Trial Balance
December 31, 19___

GENERAL JOURNAL

DATE	ACCOUNT TITLES AND EXPLANATION	P.R.	DEBIT	CREDIT

DATE	ACCOUNT TITLES AND EXPLANATION	P.R.	DEBIT	CREDIT

Merchandise Inventory

DATE	EXPLANATION	P.R.	DEBIT	CREDIT	BALANCE

(The work sheet for this problem is in the back of this booklet.)

GENERAL JOURNAL

DATE	ACCOUNT TITLES AND EXPLANATION	P.R.	DEBIT	CREDIT

DATE	ACCOUNT TITLES AND EXPLANATION	P.R.	DEBIT	CREDIT

Merchandise Inventory

DATE	EXPLANATION	P.R.	DEBIT	CREDIT	BALANCE

(The work sheet for this problem is in the back of this booklet.)

GENERAL JOURNAL

DATE	ACCOUNT TITLES AND EXPLANATION	P.R.	DEBIT	CREDIT

Merchandise Inventory

DATE	EXPLANATION	P.R.	DEBIT	CREDIT	BALANCE

(Not used for
Problem 5-3A)

WESTERN STORE, INC.
Statement of Income and Retained Earnings
For Year Ended December 31, 19___

(The work sheet for this problem is in the back of this booklet.)

GENERAL JOURNAL

DATE	ACCOUNT TITLES AND EXPLANATION	P.R.	DEBIT	CREDIT

DATE	ACCOUNT TITLES AND EXPLANATION	P.R.	DEBIT	CREDIT

(The work sheet for this problem is in the back of this booklet.)

GENERAL JOURNAL

DATE	ACCOUNT TITLES AND EXPLANATION	P.R.	DEBIT	CREDIT

DATE	ACCOUNT TITLES AND EXPLANATION	P.R.	DEBIT	CREDIT

DATE	ACCOUNT TITLES AND EXPLANATION	P.R.	DEBIT	CREDIT

DATE	ACCOUNT TITLES AND EXPLANATION	P.R.	DEBIT	CREDIT

SALES JOURNAL

DATE	ACCOUNT DEBITED	INVOICE NUMBER	P.R.	AMOUNT

CASH RECEIPTS JOURNAL

DATE	ACCOUNT CREDITED	EXPLANATION	P.R.	OTHER ACCOUNTS CREDIT	ACCOUNTS RECEIVABLE CREDIT	SALES CREDIT	SALES DISCOUNTS DEBIT	CASH DEBIT

GENERAL LEDGER
Cash   ACCT. NO. 111

DATE	EXPLANATION	P.R.	DEBIT	CREDIT	BALANCE

Accounts Receivable   ACCT. NO. 112

DATE	EXPLANATION	P.R.	DEBIT	CREDIT	BALANCE

Notes Payable   ACCT. NO. 211

DATE	EXPLANATION	P.R.	DEBIT	CREDIT	BALANCE

Sales   ACCT. NO. 411

DATE	EXPLANATION	P.R.	DEBIT	CREDIT	BALANCE

Sales Discounts   ACCT. NO. 413

DATE	EXPLANATION	P.R.	DEBIT	CREDIT	BALANCE

ACCOUNTS RECEIVABLE LEDGER

NAME *James Asner*

ADDRESS *1008 High Street*

DATE		EXPLANATION	P.R.	DEBIT	CREDIT	BALANCE

NAME *Sharon Gable*

ADDRESS *1217 Alder Street*

DATE		EXPLANATION	P.R.	DEBIT	CREDIT	BALANCE

NAME *Darla Tilman*

ADDRESS *507 East 10th Street*

DATE		EXPLANATION	P.R.	DEBIT	CREDIT	BALANCE

PURCHASES JOURNAL

DATE	ACCOUNT CREDITED	DATE OF INVOICE	TERMS	P.R.	ACCOUNTS PAYABLE CREDIT	PURCHASES DEBIT	STORE SUPPLIES DEBIT	OFFICE SUPPLIES DEBIT

CASH DISBURSEMENTS JOURNAL

DATE	CH. NO.	PAYEE	ACCOUNT DEBITED	P.R.	OTHER ACCOUNTS DEBIT	ACCOUNTS PAYABLE DEBIT	PURCHASES DISCOUNTS CREDIT	CASH CREDIT

GENERAL JOURNAL

DATE	ACCOUNT TITLES AND EXPLANATION	P.R.	DEBIT	CREDIT

GENERAL LEDGER

Cash   ACCT. NO. 111

DATE	EXPLANATION	P.R.	DEBIT	CREDIT	BALANCE

Store Supplies   ACCT. NO. 115

DATE	EXPLANATION	P.R.	DEBIT	CREDIT	BALANCE

Office Supplies   ACCT. NO. 116

DATE	EXPLANATION	P.R.	DEBIT	CREDIT	BALANCE

Store Equipment   ACCT. NO. 131

DATE	EXPLANATION	P.R.	DEBIT	CREDIT	BALANCE

Notes Payable   ACCT. NO. 211

DATE	EXPLANATION	P.R.	DEBIT	CREDIT	BALANCE

Accounts Payable   ACCT. NO. 212

DATE	EXPLANATION	P.R.	DEBIT	CREDIT	BALANCE

Purchases   ACCT. NO. 511

DATE	EXPLANATION	P.R.	DEBIT	CREDIT	BALANCE

Purchases Returns and Allowance   ACCT. NO. 512

DATE	EXPLANATION	P.R.	DEBIT	CREDIT	BALANCE

Purchases Discounts   ACCT. NO. 513

DATE	EXPLANATION	P.R.	DEBIT	CREDIT	BALANCE

Sales Salaries Expense   ACCT. NO. 612

DATE	EXPLANATION	P.R.	DEBIT	CREDIT	BALANCE

Advertising Expense   ACCT. NO. 615

DATE	EXPLANATION	P.R.	DEBIT	CREDIT	BALANCE

ACCOUNTS PAYABLE LEDGER

NAME *Casner Company*

ADDRESS *Cranston, Illinois*

DATE	EXPLANATION	P.R.	DEBIT	CREDIT	BALANCE

NAME *Lang Company*

ADDRESS *Derby, Ohio*

DATE	EXPLANATION	P.R.	DEBIT	CREDIT	BALANCE

NAME *Mason Company*

ADDRESS *Gosport, Indiana*

DATE	EXPLANATION	P.R.	DEBIT	CREDIT	BALANCE

NAME *Seattle Company*

ADDRESS *32nd and Maple*

DATE	EXPLANATION	P.R.	DEBIT	CREDIT	BALANCE

DATE		ACCOUNT DEBITED	INVOICE NUMBER	P.R.	AMOUNT
19— Jul.	7	Tom Nixon	553	√	2430 00
	16	Sheila Barnes	554	√	2700 00
	19	Jack Short	555	√	2295 00

PURCHASES JOURNAL

DATE		ACCOUNT CREDITED	DATE OF INVOICE	TERMS	P.R.	ACCOUNTS PAYABLE CREDIT	PURCHASES DEBIT	STORE SUPPLIES DEBIT	OFFICE SUPPLIES DEBIT
19— Jul.	3	Norton Company	7/2	2/10, n/60	√	2400 00	2400 00		
	6	Taft Suppliers	7/4	n/10, EOM	√	1095 00	900 00	120 00	75 00
	18	Norton Company	7/16	2/10, n/60	√	2955 00	2955 00		
	19	Able Company	7/17	2/10, n/60	√	1950 00	1950 00		

CASH RECEIPTS JOURNAL

DATE	ACCOUNT CREDITED	EXPLANATION	P.R.	OTHER ACCOUNTS CREDIT	ACCOUNTS RECEIVABLE CREDIT	SALES CREDIT	SALES DISCOUNTS DEBIT	CASH DEBIT
19— Jul. 3	Roger Nesland	Invoice 6/23	✓		3150 00		63 00	3087 00
15	Sales	Cash sales	✓			28770 00		28770 00
17	Tom Nixon	Invoice 7/7	✓		1800 00		36 00	1764 00

CASH DISBURSEMENTS JOURNAL

DATE	CH. NO.	PAYEE	ACCOUNT DEBITED	P.R.	OTHER ACCOUNTS DEBIT	ACCOUNTS PAYABLE DEBIT	PURCHASES DISCOUNTS CREDIT	CASH CREDIT
19— Jul. 1	811	Realty Mgt. Co.	Rent Expense	612	1500 00			1500 00
7	812	Best Company		✓		2850 00	57 00	2793 00
13	813	Norton Company		✓		2400 00	48 00	2352 00
15	814	David Malone	Sales Salaries Expense	611	960 00			960 00

GENERAL JOURNAL   PAGE 3

DATE		ACCOUNT TITLES AND EXPLANATION	P.R.	DEBIT	CREDIT
19— Jul.	5	Accounts Payable—Best Company	211/√	3 4 5 00	
		Purchases Returns and Allowances	512		3 4 5 00
		Returned unsatisfactory merchandise.			
	10	Sales Returns and Allowances	412	6 3 0 00	
		Accounts Receivable—Tom Nixon	112/√		6 3 0 00
		Returned merchandise.			

ACCOUNTS RECEIVABLE LEDGER

NAME **Sheila Barnes**
ADDRESS **615 First Street**

DATE		EXPLANATION	P.R.	DEBIT	CREDIT	BALANCE
19— Jul.	16		S3	2 7 0 0 00		2 7 0 0 00

NAME **Roger Nesland**
ADDRESS **1316 2nd Avenue North**

DATE		EXPLANATION	P.R.	DEBIT	CREDIT	BALANCE
19— June	23		S2	3 1 5 0 00		3 1 5 0 00
Jul.	3		R3		3 1 5 0 00	- 0 -

NAME *Tom Nixon*
ADDRESS *15 Weston Avenue*

DATE		EXPLANATION	P.R.	DEBIT	CREDIT	BALANCE
19— Jul.	7		S3	2 4 3 0 00		2 4 3 0 00
	10		G2		6 3 0 00	1 8 0 0 00
	17		R3		1 8 0 0 00	- 0 -

NAME *Jack Short*
ADDRESS *1442 Beck Street*

DATE		EXPLANATION	P.R.	DEBIT	CREDIT	BALANCE
19— Jul.	19		S3	2 2 9 5 00		2 2 9 5 00

ACCOUNTS PAYABLE LEDGER

NAME *Able Company*
ADDRESS *207 North 22nd Street*

DATE		EXPLANATION	P.R.	DEBIT	CREDIT	BALANCE
19— Jul.	19		P2		1 9 5 0 00	1 9 5 0 00

NAME *Best Company*
ADDRESS *105 Central Anenue*

DATE		EXPLANATION	P.R.	DEBIT	CREDIT	BALANCE
19— June	28		P1		3 1 9 5 00	3 1 9 5 00
Jul.	5		G2	3 4 5 00		2 8 5 0 00
	7		D4	2 8 5 0 00		- 0 -

NAME *Norton Company*

ADDRESS *2711 Walnut*

DATE		EXPLANATION	P.R.	DEBIT	CREDIT	BALANCE
19— Jul.	3		P2		2400 00	2400 00
	13		D4	2400 00		- 0 -
	18		P2		2955 00	2955 00

NAME *Taft Suppliers*

ADDRESS *137 Oak Street*

DATE		EXPLANATION	P.R.	DEBIT	CREDIT	BALANCE
19— Jul.	6		P2		1095 00	1095 00

GENERAL LEDGER

Cash   ACCT. NO. 111

DATE		EXPLANATION	P.R.	DEBIT	CREDIT	BALANCE
19— June	30	Balance	√			3930 00

Accounts Receivable   ACCT. NO. 112

DATE		EXPLANATION	P.R.	DEBIT	CREDIT	BALANCE
19— June	30	Balance	√			3150 00
Jul.	10		G2		630 00	2520 00

Merchandise Inventory

ACCT. NO. 113

DATE		EXPLANATION	P.R.	DEBIT	CREDIT	BALANCE
19— June	30	Balance	√			49 3 6 5 00

Store Supplies

ACCT. NO. 114

DATE		EXPLANATION	P.R.	DEBIT	CREDIT	BALANCE
19— June	30	Balance	√			4 5 0 00

Office Supplies

ACCT. NO. 115

DATE		EXPLANATION	P.R.	DEBIT	CREDIT	BALANCE
19— June	30	Balance	√			2 5 5 00

Store Equipment

ACCT. NO. 131

DATE		EXPLANATION	P.R.	DEBIT	CREDIT	BALANCE
19— June	30		√			35 5 6 5 00

Accumulated Depreciation, Store Equipment

ACCT. NO. 132

DATE		EXPLANATION	P.R.	DEBIT	CREDIT	BALANCE
19— June	30	Balance	√			6 7 8 0 00

Accounts Payable

ACCT. NO. 211

DATE		EXPLANATION	P.R.	DEBIT	CREDIT	BALANCE
19— June	30	Balance	√			3 1 9 5 00
Jul.	5		G2	3 4 5 00		2 8 5 0 00

Sally Fowler, Capital

ACCT. NO. 311

DATE		EXPLANATION	P.R.	DEBIT	CREDIT	BALANCE
19— June	30	Balance	√			82 7 4 0 00

Sally Fowler, Withdrawals

ACCT. NO. 312

DATE		EXPLANATION	P.R.	DEBIT	CREDIT	BALANCE

Sales

ACCT. NO. 411

DATE		EXPLANATION	P.R.	DEBIT	CREDIT	BALANCE

Sales Returns and Allowances

ACCT. NO. 412

DATE		EXPLANATION	P.R.	DEBIT	CREDIT	BALANCE
19— Jul.	10		G2	6 3 0 00		6 3 0 00

Sales Discounts

ACCT. NO. 413

DATE		EXPLANATION	P.R.	DEBIT	CREDIT	BALANCE

Purchases   ACCT. NO. 511

DATE	EXPLANATION	P.R.	DEBIT	CREDIT	BALANCE

Purchases Returns and Allowance   ACCT. NO. 512

DATE	EXPLANATION	P.R.	DEBIT	CREDIT	BALANCE
19— Jul. 5		G2		345 00	345 00

Purchases Discounts   ACCT. NO. 513

DATE	EXPLANATION	P.R.	DEBIT	CREDIT	BALANCE

Sales Salaries Expense   ACCT. NO. 611

DATE	EXPLANATION	P.R.	DEBIT	CREDIT	BALANCE
19— Jul. 15		D4	960 00		960 00

Rent Expense   ACCT. NO. 612

DATE	EXPLANATION	P.R.	DEBIT	CREDIT	BALANCE
19— Jul. 1		D4	1500 00		1500 00

Utilities Expense   ACCT. NO. 613

DATE	EXPLANATION	P.R.	DEBIT	CREDIT	BALANCE

SALES JOURNAL

DATE	ACCOUNT DEBITED	INVOICE NUMBER	P.R.	AMOUNT

PURCHASES JOURNAL

DATE	ACCOUNT CREDITED	DATE OF INVOICE	TERMS	P.R.	ACCOUNTS PAYABLE CREDIT	PURCHASES DEBIT	STORE SUPPLIES DEBIT	OFFICE SUPPLIES DEBIT

CASH RECEIPTS JOURNAL

DATE	ACCOUNT CREDITED	EXPLANATION	P.R.	OTHER ACCOUNTS CREDIT	ACCOUNTS RECEIVABLE CREDIT	SALES CREDIT	SALES DISCOUNTS DEBIT	CASH DEBIT

CASH DISBURSEMENTS JOURNAL

DATE	CH. NO.	PAYEE	ACCOUNT DEBITED	P.R.	OTHER ACCOUNTS DEBIT	ACCOUNTS PAYABLE DEBIT	PURCHASES DISCOUNTS CREDIT	CASH CREDIT

GENERAL JOURNAL

DATE	ACCOUNT TITLES AND EXPLANATION	P.R.	DEBIT	CREDIT

GENERAL JOURNAL

Cash

ACCT. NO. 111

DATE	EXPLANATION	P.R.	DEBIT	CREDIT	BALANCE

Accounts Receivable

ACCT. NO. 112

DATE	EXPLANATION	P.R.	DEBIT	CREDIT	BALANCE

Store Supplies

ACCT. NO. 115

DATE	EXPLANATION	P.R.	DEBIT	CREDIT	BALANCE

Office Supplies

ACCT. NO. 116

DATE	EXPLANATION	P.R.	DEBIT	CREDIT	BALANCE

Office Equipment

ACCT. NO. 133

DATE	EXPLANATION	P.R.	DEBIT	CREDIT	BALANCE

Notes Payable

ACCT. NO. 211

DATE	EXPLANATION	P.R.	DEBIT	CREDIT	BALANCE

Accounts Payable

ACCT. NO. 212

DATE	EXPLANATION	P.R.	DEBIT	CREDIT	BALANCE

Sales

ACCT. NO. 411

DATE	EXPLANATION	P.R.	DEBIT	CREDIT	BALANCE

Sales Discounts

ACCT. NO. 413

DATE	EXPLANATION	P.R.	DEBIT	CREDIT	BALANCE

Purchases

ACCT. NO. 511

DATE	EXPLANATION	P.R.	DEBIT	CREDIT	BALANCE

Purchases Returns and Allowances   ACCT. NO. 512

DATE	EXPLANATION	P.R.	DEBIT	CREDIT	BALANCE

Purchases Discounts   ACCT. NO. 513

DATE	EXPLANATION	P.R.	DEBIT	CREDIT	BALANCE

Sales Salaries Expense   ACCT. NO. 612

DATE	EXPLANATION	P.R.	DEBIT	CREDIT	BALANCE

ACCOUNTS RECEIVABLE LEDGER

NAME *Harry Ost*
ADDRESS *1412 West 24th Street*

DATE	EXPLANATION	P.R.	DEBIT	CREDIT	BALANCE

NAME *Kevin Stone*
ADDRESS *4314 East Oak Avenue*

DATE	EXPLANATION	P.R.	DEBIT	CREDIT	BALANCE

NAME *Shirley Tucker*

ADDRESS *3434 West 18th Street*

	DATE	EXPLANATION	P.R.	DEBIT	CREDIT	BALANCE

ACCOUNTS PAYABLE LEDGER

NAME *Intelcomp Company*

ADDRESS *1212 Ninth Avenue*

	DATE	EXPLANATION	P.R.	DEBIT	CREDIT	BALANCE

NAME *Nagle Company*

ADDRESS *15th and Oak*

	DATE	EXPLANATION	P.R.	DEBIT	CREDIT	BALANCE

NAME *Newland Company*

ADDRESS *1412 East Maple Avenue*

	DATE	EXPLANATION	P.R.	DEBIT	CREDIT	BALANCE

NAME *Slater Company*

ADDRESS *32nd and Maple*

	DATE	EXPLANATION	P.R.	DEBIT	CREDIT	BALANCE

PAGE 3

SALES JOURNAL

DATE	ACCOUNT DEBITED	INVOICE NUMBER	P.R.	AMOUNT

PAGE 3

PURCHASES JOURNAL

DATE	ACCOUNT CREDITED	DATE OF INVOICE	TERMS	P.R.	ACCOUNTS PAYABLE CREDIT	PURCHASES DEBIT	STORE SUPPLIES DEBIT	OFFICE SUPPLIES DEBIT

CASH RECEIPTS JOURNAL

DATE	ACCOUNT CREDITED	EXPLANATION	P.R.	OTHER ACCOUNTS CREDIT	ACCOUNTS RECEIVABLE CREDIT	SALES CREDIT	SALES DISCOUNTS DEBIT	CASH DEBIT

CASH DISBURSEMENTS JOURNAL

DATE	CH. NO.	PAYEE	ACCOUNT DEBITED	P.R.	OTHER ACCOUNTS DEBIT	ACCOUNTS PAYABLE DEBIT	PURCHASES DISCOUNTS CREDIT	CASH CREDIT

GENERAL JOURNAL

DATE	ACCOUNT TITLES AND EXPLANATION	P.R.	DEBIT	CREDIT

ACCOUNTS RECEIVABLE LEDGER

NAME *Charles Beckwith*

ADDRESS *1412 West 24th Street*

DATE	EXPLANATION	P.R.	DEBIT	CREDIT	BALANCE

NAME *Bob Hodges*

ADDRESS *3434 West 18th Street*

DATE	EXPLANATION	P.R.	DEBIT	CREDIT	BALANCE

NAME *Janis Shoop*

ADDRESS *4314 East Oak Avenue*

DATE	EXPLANATION	P.R.	DEBIT	CREDIT	BALANCE

ACCOUNTS PAYABLE LEDGER

NAME *Allen Company*

ADDRESS *1010 West 10th Street*

DATE	EXPLANATION	P.R.	DEBIT	CREDIT	BALANCE

NAME *Humboldt Company*

ADDRESS *711 East 15th Street*

DATE	EXPLANATION	P.R.	DEBIT	CREDIT	BALANCE

NAME *Lockhart Company*

ADDRESS *15th and Oak*

DATE	EXPLANATION	P.R.	DEBIT	CREDIT	BALANCE

NAME *Transfer Company*

ADDRESS *1412 West 24th Street*

DATE	EXPLANATION	P.R.	DEBIT	CREDIT	BALANCE

GENERAL LEDGER

Cash   ACCT. NO. 111

DATE	EXPLANATION	P.R.	DEBIT	CREDIT	BALANCE

Accounts Receivable   ACCT. NO. 112

DATE	EXPLANATION	P.R.	DEBIT	CREDIT	BALANCE

Store Supplies   ACCT. NO. 115

DATE	EXPLANATION	P.R.	DEBIT	CREDIT	BALANCE

Office Supplies   ACCT. NO. 116

DATE	EXPLANATION	P.R.	DEBIT	CREDIT	BALANCE

Store Equipment   ACCT. NO. 131

DATE	EXPLANATION	P.R.	DEBIT	CREDIT	BALANCE

Accounts Payable   ACCT. NO. 212

DATE		EXPLANATION	P.R.	DEBIT	CREDIT	BALANCE

Sales   ACCT. NO. 411

DATE		EXPLANATION	P.R.	DEBIT	CREDIT	BALANCE

Sales Returns and Allowances   ACCT. NO. 412

DATE		EXPLANATION	P.R.	DEBIT	CREDIT	BALANCE

Sales Discounts   ACCT. NO. 413

DATE		EXPLANATION	P.R.	DEBIT	CREDIT	BALANCE

Purchases   ACCT. NO. 511

DATE		EXPLANATION	P.R.	DEBIT	CREDIT	BALANCE

Purchases Returns and Allowances   ACCT. NO. 512

DATE		EXPLANATION	P.R.	DEBIT	CREDIT	BALANCE

Purchases Discounts   ACCT. NO. 513

DATE		EXPLANATION	P.R.	DEBIT	CREDIT	BALANCE

Sales Salaries Expense   ACCT. NO. 612

DATE		EXPLANATION	P.R.	DEBIT	CREDIT	BALANCE

Advertising Expense   ACCT. NO. 615

DATE		EXPLANATION	P.R.	DEBIT	CREDIT	BALANCE

PAGE 2

PURCHASES JOURNAL

DATE	ACCOUNT DEBITED	INVOICE NUMBER	P.R.	AMOUNT

DATE	ACCOUNT CREDITED	DATE OF INVOICE	TERMS	P.R.	ACCOUNTS PAYABLE CREDIT	PURCHASES DEBIT	STORE SUPPLIES DEBIT	OFFICE SUPPLIES DEBIT

CASH RECEIPTS JOURNAL

PAGE 2

DATE	ACCOUNT CREDITED	EXPLANATION	P.R.	OTHER ACCOUNTS CREDIT	ACCOUNTS RECEIVABLE CREDIT	SALES CREDIT	SALES DISCOUNTS DEBIT	CASH DEBIT

CASH DISBURSEMENTS JOURNAL

PAGE 2

DATE	CH. NO.	PAYEE	ACCOUNT DEBITED	P.R.	OTHER ACCOUNTS DEBIT	ACCOUNTS PAYABLE DEBIT	PURCHASES DISCOUNTS CREDIT	CASH CREDIT

BRAVO COMPANY (Continued) Name _____

DATE	ACCOUNT TITLES AND EXPLANATION	P.R.	DEBIT	CREDIT

DATE	ACCOUNT TITLES AND EXPLANATION	P.R.	DEBIT	CREDIT

(This work sheet for this problem is on page 292.)

GENERAL LEDGER

Cash   ACCT. NO. 111

DATE		EXPLANATION	P.R.	DEBIT	CREDIT	BALANCE
19— May	31	Balance	√			6 8 5 0 00

Accounts Receivable   ACCT. NO. 112

DATE		EXPLANATION	P.R.	DEBIT	CREDIT	BALANCE
19— May	31	Balance	√			2 9 5 0 00

Merchandise Inventory   ACCT. NO. 113

DATE		EXPLANATION	P.R.	DEBIT	CREDIT	BALANCE
19— May	31	Balance	√			27 4 5 0 00

Prepaid Insurance   ACCT. NO. 114

DATE		EXPLANATION	P.R.	DEBIT	CREDIT	BALANCE
19— May	31	Balance	√			1 3 6 0 00

Store Supplies   ACCT. NO. 115

DATE		EXPLANATION	P.R.	DEBIT	CREDIT	BALANCE
19— May	31	Balance	√			4 7 0 00

Office Supplies   ACCT. NO. 116

DATE		EXPLANATION	P.R.	DEBIT	CREDIT	BALANCE
19— May	31	Balance	√			2 9 0 00

Store Equipment   ACCT. NO. 131

DATE		EXPLANATION	P.R.	DEBIT	CREDIT	BALANCE
19— May	31	Balance	√			17 8 0 0 00

Accumulated Depreciation, Store Equipment   ACCT. NO. 132

DATE		EXPLANATION	P.R.	DEBIT	CREDIT	BALANCE
19— May	31	Balance	√			4 9 0 0 00

Office Equipment   ACCT. NO. 133

DATE		EXPLANATION	P.R.	DEBIT	CREDIT	BALANCE
19— May	31	Balance	√			9 2 0 0 00

Accumulated Depreciation, Office Equipment   ACCT. NO. 134

DATE		EXPLANATION	P.R.	DEBIT	CREDIT	BALANCE
19— May	31	Balance	√			3 2 0 0 00

Accounts Payable   ACCT. NO. 212

DATE		EXPLANATION	P.R.	DEBIT	CREDIT	BALANCE
19— May	31	Balance	√			2 3 6 0 00

Ralph Weber, Capital   ACCT. NO. 311

DATE		EXPLANATION	P.R.	DEBIT	CREDIT	BALANCE
19— May	31	Balance	√			55 9 1 0 00

Ralph Weber, Withdrawals   ACCT. NO. 312

DATE	EXPLANATION	P.R.	DEBIT	CREDIT	BALANCE

Income Summary   ACCT. NO. 313

DATE	EXPLANATION	P.R.	DEBIT	CREDIT	BALANCE

Sales   ACCT. NO. 411

DATE	EXPLANATION	P.R.	DEBIT	CREDIT	BALANCE

Sales Returns and Allowances   ACCT. NO. 412

DATE	EXPLANATION	P.R.	DEBIT	CREDIT	BALANCE

Sales Discounts   ACCT. NO. 413

DATE	EXPLANATION	P.R.	DEBIT	CREDIT	BALANCE

Purchases   ACCT. NO. 511

DATE	EXPLANATION	P.R.	DEBIT	CREDIT	BALANCE

Purchases Returns and Allowances   ACCT. NO. 512

DATE		EXPLANATION	P.R.	DEBIT	CREDIT	BALANCE

Purchases Discounts   ACCT. NO. 513

DATE		EXPLANATION	P.R.	DEBIT	CREDIT	BALANCE

Sales Salaries Expense   ACCT. NO. 611

DATE		EXPLANATION	P.R.	DEBIT	CREDIT	BALANCE

Rent Expense, Selling Space   ACCT. NO. 612

DATE		EXPLANATION	P.R.	DEBIT	CREDIT	BALANCE

Store Supplies Expense   ACCT. NO. 613

DATE		EXPLANATION	P.R.	DEBIT	CREDIT	BALANCE

Depreciation Expense, Store Equipment   ACCT. NO. 614

DATE		EXPLANATION	P.R.	DEBIT	CREDIT	BALANCE

Office Salaries Expense   ACCT. NO. 651

DATE		EXPLANATION	P.R.	DEBIT	CREDIT	BALANCE

Rent Expense, Office Space   ACCT. NO. 652

DATE		EXPLANATION	P.R.	DEBIT	CREDIT	BALANCE

Insurance Expense   ACCT. NO. 653

DATE		EXPLANATION	P.R.	DEBIT	CREDIT	BALANCE

Office Supplies Expense   ACCT. NO. 654

DATE		EXPLANATION	P.R.	DEBIT	CREDIT	BALANCE

Depreciation Expense, Office Equipment   ACCT. NO. 655

DATE		EXPLANATION	P.R.	DEBIT	CREDIT	BALANCE

Utilities Expense   ACCT. NO. 656

DATE		EXPLANATION	P.R.	DEBIT	CREDIT	BALANCE

ACCOUNTS RECEIVABLE LEDGER

NAME *Berry Company*
ADDRESS *1212 North Bay*

DATE		EXPLANATION	P.R.	DEBIT	CREDIT	BALANCE
19—May	31		S1	2 9 5 0 00		2 9 5 0 00

NAME *Mayfield Constructors*
ADDRESS *2000 Industry Road*

DATE	EXPLANATION	P.R.	DEBIT	CREDIT	BALANCE

NAME *Nate's Repairs*
ADDRESS *407 North 15th Street*

DATE	EXPLANATION	P.R.	DEBIT	CREDIT	BALANCE

NAME *Tisdale Company*
ADDRESS *124 Washington Anenue*

DATE	EXPLANATION	P.R.	DEBIT	CREDIT	BALANCE

ACCOUNTS PAYABLE LEDGER

NAME *Easton Suppliers*

ADDRESS *7300 Falcon Ledge*

DATE	EXPLANATION	P.R.	DEBIT	CREDIT	BALANCE

NAME *Goodman Products*

ADDRESS *13 Oakdale*

DATE	EXPLANATION	P.R.	DEBIT	CREDIT	BALANCE
19— May 31				2 3 6 0 00	2 3 6 0 00

NAME *Settle Brothers*

ADDRESS *1212 Castle Ridge*

DATE	EXPLANATION	P.R.	DEBIT	CREDIT	BALANCE

NAME *Ulrich Materials*

ADDRESS *725 St. Johns Boulevard*

DATE	EXPLANATION	P.R.	DEBIT	CREDIT	BALANCE

BRAVO COMPANY

Income Statement

For Month Ended June 30, 19--

BRAVO COMPANY

Balance Sheet

June 30, 19--

BRAVO COMPANY (Continued)

BRAVO COMPANY
Post-closing Trial Balance
June 30, 19--

BRAVO COMPANY
Schedule of Accounts Receivable
June 30, 19--

BRAVO COMPANY
Schedule of Accounts Payable
June 30, 19--

Part 1

GENERAL JOURNAL

DATE	ACCOUNT TITLES AND EXPLANATION	P.R.	DEBIT	CREDIT

Part 2

DATE	ACCOUNT TITLES AND EXPLANATION	P.R.	DEBIT	CREDIT

Part 1   GENERAL JOURNAL

DATE	ACCOUNT TITLES AND EXPLANATION	P.R.	DEBIT	CREDIT

Part 2

Part 3

DATE		ACCOUNT TITLES AND EXPLANATION	P.R.	DEBIT	CREDIT

Part 1

DATE	ACCOUNT TITLES AND EXPLANATION	P.R.	DEBIT	CREDIT

GENERAL JOURNAL

DATE	ACCOUNT TITLES AND EXPLANATION	P.R.	DEBIT	CREDIT

DATE	ACCOUNT TITLES AND EXPLANATION	P.R.	DEBIT	CREDIT

Part 1, (a)

DATE	ACCOUNT TITLES AND EXPLANATION	P.R.	DEBIT	CREDIT

Part 1, (b)

Part 2, (a)

DATE	ACCOUNT TITLES AND EXPLANATION	P.R.	DEBIT	CREDIT

PAGE 5   *Voucher*

	Date	Vchr. No.	Payee	When and How Paid		Vouchers Payable Credit	Purchases Debit	Transportation-In Debit	
				Date	Ch. No.				
1									1
2									2
3									3
4									4
5									5
6									6
7									7
8									8
9									9
10									10

Register   PAGE 5

	Sales Salaries Expense Debit	Advertising Expense Debit	Office Salaries Expense Debit	Other Accounts Debit			
				Account Name	P.R.	Amount	
1							1
2							2
3							3
4							4
5							5
6							6
7							7
8							8
9							9
10							10

Check Register   PAGE 5

Date	Payee	Vchr. No.	Ch. No.	Vouchers Payable Dr.	Purchases Discount Cr.	Cash Cr.

GENERAL JOURNAL

DATE	ACCOUNT TITLES AND EXPLANATION	P.R.	DEBIT	CREDIT

Vouchers Payable   ACCT. No. 212

DATE	EXPLANATION	P.R.	DEBIT	CREDIT	BALANCE

VOUCHER NUMBER	PAYEE	AMOUNT

GENERAL JOURNAL

DATE		ACCOUNT TITLES AND EXPLANATION	P.R.	DEBIT	CREDIT

DATE	ACCOUNT TITLES AND EXPLANATION	P.R.	DEBIT	CREDIT

Part 1

GENERAL JOURNAL

DATE	ACCOUNT TITLES AND EXPLANATION	P.R.	DEBIT	CREDIT

Part 2

Part 3

Part 1

Part 2

GENERAL JOURNAL

DATE	ACCOUNT TITLES AND EXPLANATION	P.R.	DEBIT	CREDIT

GENERAL JOURNAL   **PAGE 1**

DATE		ACCOUNT TITLES AND EXPLANATION	P.R.	DEBIT	CREDIT

DATE	ACCOUNT TITLES AND EXPLANATION	P.R.	DEBIT	CREDIT

GENERAL JOURNAL   **PAGE 1**

DATE	ACCOUNT TITLES AND EXPLANATION	P.R.	DEBIT	CREDIT

DATE		ACCOUNT TITLES AND EXPLANATION	P.R.	DEBIT	CREDIT

GENERAL JOURNAL

DATE	ACCOUNT TITLES AND EXPLANATION	P.R.	DEBIT	CREDIT

DATE		ACCOUNT TITLES AND EXPLANATION	P.R.	DEBIT	CREDIT	

Interest Receivable   ACCT. NO. 113

DATE		EXPLANATION	P.R.	DEBIT	CREDIT	BALANCE

Allowance for Doubtful Accounts   ACCT. NO. 115

DATE		EXPLANATION	P.R.	DEBIT	CREDIT	BALANCE

Bad Debts Expense   ACCT. NO. 651

DATE		EXPLANATION	P.R.	DEBIT	CREDIT	BALANCE

Interest Earned   ACCT. NO. 711

DATE		EXPLANATION	P.R.	DEBIT	CREDIT	BALANCE

	FIFO	LIFO	WEIGHTED-AVERAGE COST
Sales			
Cost of goods sold:			
Inventory, January 1, 19___			
Purchases			
Goods available for sale			
Inventory, December 31, 19___			
Cost of goods sold			
Gross profit on sales			
Operating expenses			
Net income			

Case 1

Product	Units on Hand	Per Unit Cost	Market	Total Cost	Total Market	Lower of Cost or Market (by product)

_____

_____

_____

_____

_____

_____

Case 2

_____

Product	Units on Hand	Per Unit Cost	Market	Total Cost	Total Market	Lower of Cost or Market (by product)

_____

_____

_____

_____

_____

_____

Product	Units on Hand	Per Unit		Total Cost	Total Market	Lower of Cost or Market (by product)
		Cost	Market			

	198A	198B	198C

Part 1

| Item _____ | | | Location in stockroom _____ | | | | | | | | | |
| Maximum _____ Minimum _____ | | | | | | | | | | | | |

DATE		PURCHASED				SOLD				BALANCE		
		UNITS	COST	TOTAL		UNITS	COST	TOTAL		UNITS	COST	BALANCE

Item _____	Location in stockroom _____

Maximum _____ Minimum _____

DATE		PURCHASED			SOLD			BALANCE		
		UNITS	COST	TOTAL	UNITS	COST	TOTAL	UNITS	COST	BALANCE

Part 3

DATE		ACCOUNT TITLES AND EXPLANATION	P.R.	DEBIT	CREDIT

Part 1

	Land	Building _____	Building _____	Land Improvements _____	Land Improvements _____

Parts 2 and 3

DATE	ACCOUNT TITLES AND EXPLANATION	P.R.	DEBIT	CREDIT

Part 1

Year	Straight-line	Units-of Production	Declining Balance	Sum-of-the-Years' Digits

Part 2

DATE		ACCOUNT TITLES AND EXPLANATION	P.R.	DEBIT	CREDIT

Part 1

Machine Number	198A Depre-ciation	198B Depre-ciation	198C Depre-ciation	198D Depre-ciation	198E Depre-ciation

Part 2

Plant Equipment

DATE	EXPLANATION	P.R.	DEBIT	CREDIT	BALANCE

Accumulated Depreciation, Plant Equipment

DATE	EXPLANATION	P.R.	DEBIT	CREDIT	BALANCE

SUBSIDIARY PLANT ASSET AND DEPRECIATION RECORD No. _____

Item _____

Mfg. Serial No. _____

Estimated Life _____

Depreciation per year _____

General Ledger
Account _____

Purchased
from _____

Estimated Salvage Value _____

per month _____

Date	Explanation	Asset Record			Depreciation Record		
		Debit	Credit	Balance	Debit	Credit	Balance

Final Disposition of the Asset _____

SUBSIDIARY PLANT ASSET AND DEPRECIATION RECORD No. _____

Item _____

Mfg. Serial No. _____

Estimated Life _____

Depreciation per year _____

General Ledger
Account _____

Purchased
from _____

Estimated Salvage Value _____

per month _____

Date	Explanation	Asset Record			Depreciation Record		
		Debit	Credit	Balance	Debit	Credit	Balance

Final Disposition of the Asset _____

SUBSIDIARY PLANT ASSET AND DEPRECIATION RECORD No. _____

Item _____

General Ledger
Account _____

Mfg. Serial No. _____

Purchased
from _____

Estimated Life _____

Estimated Salvage Value _____

Depreciation per year _____

per month _____

Date	Explanation	Asset Record			Depreciation Record		
		Debit	Credit	Balance	Debit	Credit	Balance

Final Disposition of the Asset _____

GENERAL JOURNAL

DATE	ACCOUNT TITLES AND EXPLANATION	P.R.	DEBIT	CREDIT

DATE	ACCOUNT TITLES AND EXPLANATION	P.R.	DEBIT	CREDIT

GENERAL JOURNAL

DATE	ACCOUNT TITLES AND EXPLANATION	P.R.	DEBIT	CREDIT

DATE	ACCOUNT TITLES AND EXPLANATION	P.R.	DEBIT	CREDIT

GENERAL JOURNAL

DATE	ACCOUNT TITLES AND EXPLANATION	P.R.	DEBIT	CREDIT

GENERAL JOURNAL

DATE	ACCOUNT TITLES AND EXPLANATION	P.R.	DEBIT	CREDIT

Part 1

DATE	ACCOUNT TITLES AND EXPLANATION	P.R.	DEBIT	CREDIT

Part 2

DATE	ACCOUNT TITLES AND EXPLANATION	P.R.	DEBIT	CREDIT

GENERAL JOURNAL

DATE		ACCOUNT TITLES AND EXPLANATION	P.R.	DEBIT	CREDIT

DATE	ACCOUNT TITLES AND EXPLANATION	P.R.	DEBIT	CREDIT

GENERAL JOURNAL

DATE	ACCOUNT TITLES AND EXPLANATION	P.R.	DEBIT	CREDIT

DATE		ACCOUNT TITLES AND EXPLANATION	P.R.	DEBIT	CREDIT

Part 1

Year	Beginning-of-Year Carrying Amount	Discount to Be Amortized Each Year	Unamortized Discount at End of Year	End-of-Year Carrying Amount

Part 2

DATE	ACCOUNT TITLES AND EXPLANATION	P.R.	DEBIT	CREDIT

Part 3

DATE		ACCOUNT TITLES AND EXPLANATION	P.R.	DEBIT	CREDIT

Part 1

Year	Beginning-of-Year Lease Liability	Beginning-of-Year Unamortized Discount	Beginning-of-Year Carrying Amount	Discount to be Amortized	Unamortized Discount at End of Year	End-of-Year Lease Liability	End-of-Year Carrying Amount

Part 2

DATE	ACCOUNT TITLES AND EXPLANATION	P.R.	DEBIT	CREDIT

DATE	ACCOUNT TITLES AND EXPLANATION	P.R.	DEBIT	CREDIT

Year	Beginning-of-Year Lease Liability	Beginning-of-Year Unamortized Discount	Beginning-of-Year Carrying Amount	Discount to be Amortized	Unamortized Discount at End of Year	End-of-Year Lease Liability	End-of-Year Carrying Amount

GENERAL JOURNAL

DATE	ACCOUNT TITLES AND EXPLANATION	P.R.	DEBIT	CREDIT

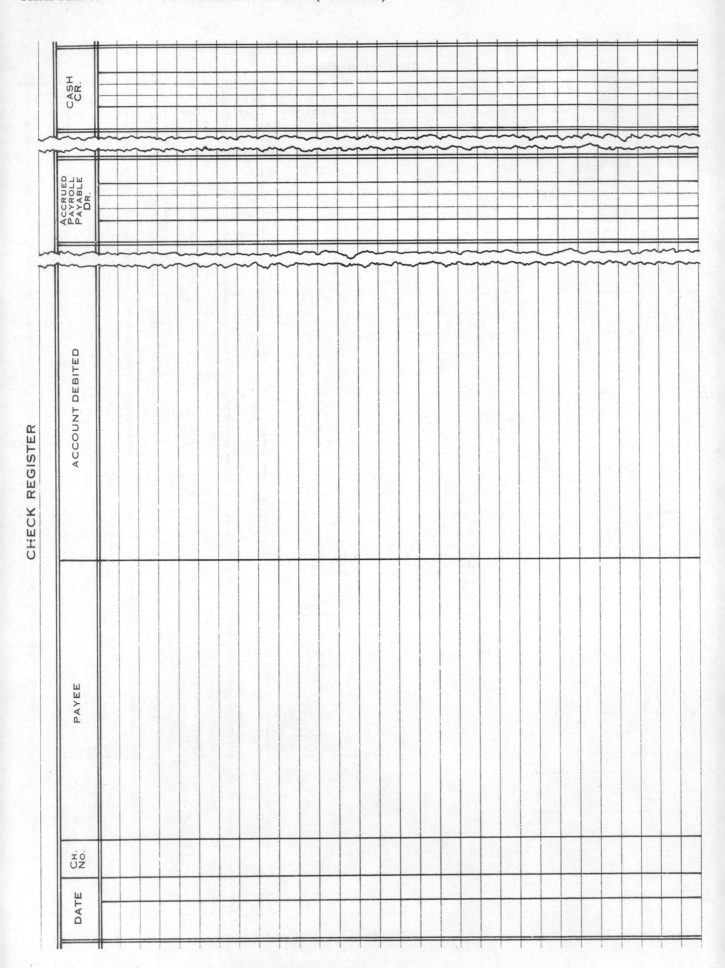

GENERAL JOURNAL

DATE	ACCOUNT TITLES AND EXPLANATION	P.R.	DEBIT	CREDIT

PAYROLL REGISTER

| EMPLOYEE | CLOCK CARD NUMBER | DAILY TIME | | | | | | | TOTAL HOURS | O.T. HOURS | REG. PAY RATE | EARNINGS | | | |
		M	T	W	T	F	S	S				REGULAR PAY	O.T. PREMIUM PAY	GROSS PAY	
															1
															2
															3
															4
															5
															6
															7
															8
															9

CHECK REGISTER

DATE	CH. No.	PAYEE	ACCOUNT DEBITED	
				1
				2
				3
				4
				5
				6
				7
				8

Week ended

	FICA TAXES		INCOME TAXES		MEDICAL INSUR-ANCE		UNION DUES		TOTAL DEDUC-TIONS		NET PAY		CHECK NUMBER	SALES SALARIES		OFFICE SALARIES		SERVICE WAGES EXPENSE	
	DEDUCTIONS										PAYMENT				DISTRIBUTION					
1																				
2																				
3																				
4																				
5																				
6																				
7																				
8																				
9																				

	P.R.	OTHER ACCOUNTS DR.	ACCOUNTS PAYABLE DR.	ACCRUED PAYROLL PAYABLE DR.	PURCHASES DISCOUNT CR.	CASH CR.
1						
2						
3						
4						
5						
6						
7						
8						

GENERAL JOURNAL

DATE	ACCOUNT TITLES AND EXPLANATION	P.R.	DEBIT	CREDIT

GENERAL JOURNAL

DATE	ACCOUNT TITLES AND EXPLANATION	P.R.	DEBIT	CREDIT

PAYROLL REGISTER

EMPLOYEE	CLOCK CARD NUMBER	DAILY TIME							TOTAL HOURS	O.T. HOURS	REG. PAY RATE	EARNINGS			
		M	T	W	T	F	S	S				REGULAR PAY	O.T. PREMIUM PAY	GROSS PAY	
															1
															2
															3
															4
															5
															6
															7
															8
															9

CHECK REGISTER

DATE	CH. NO.	PAYEE	ACCOUNT DEBITED	
				1
				2
				3
				4
				5
				6
				7
				8

Week ended

	DEDUCTIONS					PAYMENT		DISTRIBUTION		
	FICA TAXES	INCOME TAXES	MEDICAL INSUR-ANCE	UNION DUES	TOTAL DEDUC-TIONS	NET PAY	CHECK NUMBER	SALES SALARIES	OFFICE SALARIES	SHOP WAGES
1										
2										
3										
4										
5										
6										
7										
8										
9										

	P.R.	OTHER ACCOUNTS DR.	ACCOUNTS PAYABLE DR.	ACCRUED PAYROLL PAYABLE DR.	PURCHASES DISCOUNT CR.	CASH CR.
1						
2						
3						
4						
5						
6						
7						
8						

GENERAL JOURNAL

DATE	ACCOUNT TITLES AND EXPLANATION	P.R.	DEBIT	CREDIT

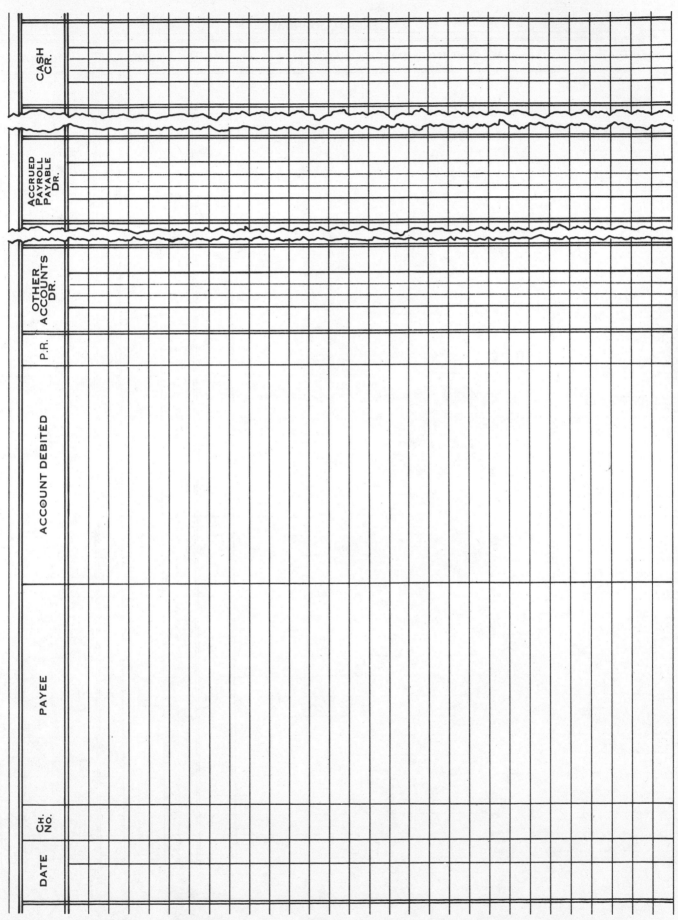

GENERAL JOURNAL

DATE	ACCOUNT TITLES AND EXPLANATION	P.R.	DEBIT	CREDIT

DATE		ACCOUNT TITLES AND EXPLANATION	P.R.	DEBIT	CREDIT

Income Sharing Plan	Year _____ Calculations						

Income Sharing Plan	Year _____ Calculations		

Income Sharing Plan	Year _____ Calculations				

Part 1

Income Sharing Plan	Calculations															

GENERAL JOURNAL   PAGE 1

DATE	ACCOUNT TITLES AND EXPLANATION	P.R.	DEBIT	CREDIT

DATE		ACCOUNT TITLES AND EXPLANATION	P.R.	DEBIT	CREDIT

GENERAL JOURNAL

DATE	ACCOUNT TITLES AND EXPLANATION	P.R.	DEBIT	CREDIT

GENERAL JOURNAL

DATE	ACCOUNT TITLES AND EXPLANATION	P.R.	DEBIT	CREDIT

GENERAL JOURNAL

DATE	ACCOUNT TITLES AND EXPLANATION	P.R.	DEBIT	CREDIT

GENERAL JOURNAL

DATE	ACCOUNT TITLES AND EXPLANATION	P.R.	DEBIT	CREDIT